INSIDE ART MOVEMENTS

Surrealism

Susie Brooks

WAYLAND
www.waylandbooks.co.uk

First published in 2018 by Wayland
Copyright © Hodder & Stoughton, 2018

Series editor: Julia Bird
Designer: Mo Choy Design Ltd.
Picture research: Diana Morris

ISBN 978 1 5263 0 6159

Printed in China

Wayland
An imprint of
Hachette Children's Group
Part of Hodder and Stoughton
Carmelite House
50 Victoria Embankment
London EC4Y 0DZ

www.hachette.co.uk

FSC
www.fsc.org
MIX
Paper from
responsible sources
FSC® C104740

Contents

Unconscious art

Try not to think of anything at all. Does something pop into your head anyway? That's your subconscious, or unknowing mind, working. The Surrealists found this idea so fascinating that they decided to use it in their art!

What is Surrealism?

Surrealism began as a writers' movement, but it quickly found its way into art. The poet André Breton, who lived in Paris, launched it in 1924 when he wrote his first *Surrealist Manifesto*. In this he talked about expressing the subconscious and rejecting rational thought (the bossy part of our brain!). He used dreams as the perfect example, because we dream without actually deciding to.

Slip of the brush

The strange, unexpected images of dreams captivated the Surrealists. If the subconscious could make them up all on its own, then they wanted the subconscious to help make their art! They tried to find ways to free their creativity and let pictures come to them without thinking. Imagine an accidental 'slip of the tongue' – but in the form of a painting.

Dutch Interior (I), Joan Miró, 1928

"When I stand before a canvas, I never know what I will do, and I am the first one surprised at what comes out."

Joan Miró

Traumatic times

Surrealism grew out of troubled times, in the aftermath of the First World War (1914–1918). Artists had been scattered and traumatised by the war, and some had begun rebelling with a style called Dada. They rejected tradition and made 'anti-art' art with illogical objects and images (see p.6). This shocked most people at the time, but delighted the Surrealists!

Surreal lives

Some Surrealist artists, including Joan Miró and André Masson, concentrated on painting 'unconsciously' (see p.12). Others, such as Salvador Dalí and René Magritte, created dream-like scenes in an ultra-realistic style. There were artists who made surreal objects, and Surrealist photographers too. Many of them also lived surreal lifestyles, doing eccentric and irrational things!

Swans Reflecting Elephants, Salvador Dalí, 1937

🖋 *Look closer*

Does this painting by Dalí remind you of a dream? What is unusual about it? Look at the shapes reflected in the water.

Hobbyhorse war

If you looked up 'dada' in a French dictionary, you'd find that it's a word for a hobbyhorse. So why did a group of artists pick it as a name? Because it had nothing to do with their art!

Attack on logic

The Dada movement was all about defying logic and reason. It sprung up in Switzerland around 1916, in the middle of the First World War. A group of young artists decided that if logic and reason were responsible for the war, then they should behave in the opposite way. They started attacking everything that art, politics and society in general stood for.

Cubism and collage

By the time the First World War broke out, art was already changing. Cubists like Pablo Picasso and Juan Gris had torn apart traditional painting and pictured the world as a jumble of geometric shapes. They also invented collage, bringing cheap, everyday materials into their work. This questioned the value of elitist 'high art' and gave the Dadaists ideas.

········▶ *Look closer*

Instead of painting what they saw in one moment, the Cubists showed things from lots of viewpoints at once, as in this painting by Juan Gris. Why do you think they did this? Can you see why their work appealed to the Dadaists?

Breakfast, Juan Gris, 1914

Absurd art

Dada spread quickly to Paris, New York and Germany, where modern art was flourishing. Raoul Haussman, of the Berlin group, made this scrap collage to ridicule snooty art critics. In New York, Marcel Duchamp drew a moustache on a copy of the *Mona Lisa* – a very famous portrait by Leonardo da Vinci – and gave it a new title. He also took ordinary objects, from bicycle wheels to urinals, called them readymades and signed them as art!

The Art Critic, Raoul Haussman, 1919-20

Bicycle Wheel, Marcel Duchamp, 1913

New meaning

The Dadaists wanted to open people's eyes to what art is and who decides. They staged provocative exhibitions, including one in a Cologne beer hall in 1920, which visitors had to enter through a public toilet. By now though, the war had ended and Dada was beginning to lose its point. The Surrealists took its disruption of everything rational and gave it new meaning, by putting it in the context of the unconscious mind.

Surreal beginnings

André Breton was part of the Dada group in Paris, but in the early 1920s his path to Surrealism began. 'Leave everything,' he said. 'Leave Dada ... leave your hopes and fears ... leave your easy life ... set off on the road.'

Dream windows

Breton was very interested in the workings of the human mind. He was a trained psychiatrist and had served in a neurological hospital during the First World War. In 1921 he visited Sigmund Freud, a pioneering Austrian doctor who believed that dreams are the window to our subconscious. Freud's groundbreaking ideas had a huge impact on Breton and Surrealism.

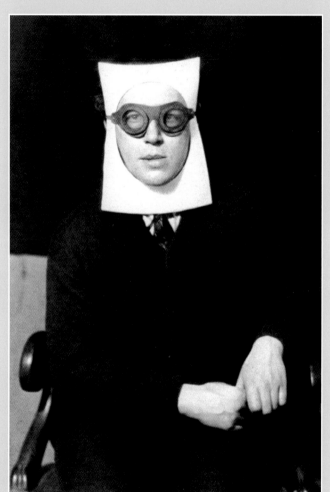

A Surrealist portrait of André Breton

Psychic automatism

When Breton wrote his *Manifesto* in 1924, he described Surrealism as 'pure psychic automatism'. He meant that it was a way to freely express the imagination, without the thinking mind getting in the way. Breton and his writer and artist friends formed an office called the Bureau of Surrealist Research. Here they held discussions and invited people to come and 'confess' things that their subconscious had made them do!

Unpredictable art

At first, Surrealist writers believed that painting and sculpting needed too much thought to be spontaneous and fresh from the subconscious. But Max Ernst, Joan Miró, André Masson and others soon proved them wrong. In 1925, the Surrealist artists held their first group exhibition in Paris. It included techniques such as 'automatic' art (see p.16) and photomontage, a type of collage invented by the Dadaists.

Vertumnus, Giuseppe Arcimboldo, c.1590–91

The Song of Love, Giorgio de Chirico, 1914

Surreal forerunners

The Surrealists admired other artists who painted 'unlikely' images. For example, Giuseppe Arcimboldo's fruit-faces of the 1500s (above) were bizarre and surprising – Surrealism ahead of its time! A strong contemporary influence was Giorgio de Chirico, who called his paintings 'metaphysical' because they showed things beyond the physical world. This creepy street, with its strange scale and random objects, looks like a vision from a dream.

Nightingale nightmare

'At nightfall, at the outskirts of the village, two children are threatened by a nightingale.' This was the start of a poem, written by Max Ernst shortly before he painted this unnerving picture.

Not as it seems

At first glance this might look like a sunny, carefree scene – but we quickly see that it isn't. One girl is wielding a knife, while another faints and a third is carried away by an adult. Ernst's painting is peculiar even in its title – there are three children here, not two. The nightingale is a tiny songbird and doesn't seem at all scary! But Ernst shows us that in a dream or nightmare, something unthreatening can be terrifying.

Mixed materials

Ernst used a mixture of real and painted elements to add to the sense of confusion. He called it a 'farewell' to the collages he had made in his Dada days (he was known as Dadamax!). Here the wooden gate welcomes us in – but what part does the knob play on the right-hand side? Is it a panic button, or a door handle to help the figures escape?

"Every normal human being ... has an inexhaustible store of buried images in his subconscious."

Max Ernst

Fevervision

Ernst said that this painting was inspired by a 'fevervision' – a hallucination that he experienced when he had measles as a child. He remembered seeing the wood grain in a panel opposite his bed take on different shapes, from an eye to a frightening bird. When he was better, he carried on 'looking' – staring at clouds, wallpapers, stonework and so on, waiting for his mind to create pictures.

Uneasy influences

Birds often appeared in Max Ernst's work. He described himself as having hatched from an egg, and gave himself a birdlike identity called 'Loplop'. His wild imagination was shaped by various events, including the death of his sister when he was young. Ernst was also deeply traumatised by fighting in the First World War, which may help to explain this disorientating painting.

Intentional accidents

Hold a pencil over some paper and let your hand just draw. The Surrealists believed this spontaneous 'automatism' would reveal something from their inner selves that they never knew was there.

Automatic action

It all began with Sigmund Freud (see p.8), who used a method called 'free association' with his patients. He hoped to tap into their unconscious minds by asking them to talk about whatever popped into their heads. Breton went on to experiment with 'automatic writing' – putting words down quickly before logic took over and made sense of them. Artists soon followed suit, with automatic drawings like Masson's (right).

Automatic Drawing, André Masson, 1924

Partly conscious

The idea of chance in art had already been explored by the Dadaists. Hans Arp, for example, made the collage on p.13 by dropping scraps of paper and (supposedly!) gluing them just where they fell. The fact that they look so orderly suggests that he did at least partly arrange them. This was often true of Surrealist automatic drawing too – artists might see shapes in the marks they made and consciously turn them into something.

Untitled (Collage with Squares Arranged According to the Laws of Chance), Jean (Hans) Arp, 1917

Exquisite Corpse

The Surrealists loved playing games, especially Exquisite Corpse. This was similar to the game of Consequences, where each person draws or writes something, folds the paper down and then passes it on to the next. It leads to an illogical final picture or sentence, created beyond anyone's control. Breton said it was like sending the critical mind on holiday!

In a trance

Sometimes the Surrealists got together and spoke, wrote or drew under hypnosis. They were fascinated by trances, sleep and other mental states where the thinking mind is subdued. They also admired art by young children and the mentally ill, because it seemed to express things freely, without any self-consciousness.

A hunger party

Strange creatures dance at a party, so lively that even the ladder and tablecloth want to join in! There's music in the air and everyone is happy – except for the hungry Harlequin.

Starving shapes

When Joan Miró painted this, he had very little money. He remembered one day when a friend came for dinner, he could only afford to serve radishes. Miró said he was so hungry that he often had hallucinations. He would see shapes on the bare walls of his studio, and these were what he put down in paint.

A hole in Harlequin

Can you spot the figure of Harlequin, towards the left of the painting? He's the one with the sad expression and a long moustache on his blue-and-red face. If you look down to his body, you can see it is shaped like a guitar. The hole in the guitar is probably a symbol of the hunger Miró was feeling. It looks as if one of the creatures is trying to feed it something!

Look closer

Harlequin was a trickster character from Italian theatre, with a chequered costume, a magic 'slapstick' and often an admiral's hat. Can you find these here? What else can you see in the painting?

A sunny carnival

Miró came from Catalonia in Spain, and he painted in the colours of his sunny native landscape. They add to the feeling of celebration in this busy picture. It is thought to be a scene of Mardi Gras, the carnival before Lent in the Christian calendar. People often dress up in bright costumes and masks, which might explain some of the strange characters here.

Magical Miró

In 1925, Miró's first solo Surrealist exhibition opened at midnight in a Paris gallery. It was a massive success, partly thanks to his cheerful, humorous style. Miró painted his fantastical images on anything he could find, from black card to metal sheets or flour sacks. Often he started them 'automatically' with random splashes of paint.

Harlequin's Carnival, Joan Miró, 1924-25

Chance experiments

In 1925, in a hotel on the coast of France, Max Ernst had a flash of inspiration. After staring at the wood grain in the floorboards of his room, he dropped some paper on them and rubbed over the surfaces with a pencil.

Floorboard frottage

Ernst called his new discovery 'frottage', which is French for 'rubbing'. He soon extended it to wire mesh, lengths of twine, crumpled paper … even bread crusts! The textures that appeared conjured up images in his mind, and he turned them into surreal scenes or creatures. In 1926, he exhibited a series of 34 frottages under the title 'Natural History'.

Scraping paint

Next, Ernst translated his technique to paint, calling it 'grattage' or 'scraping'. In a similar way he would lay a painted canvas onto wood, chair caning, fish bones or other textured material, then scrape over the surface. The point of all this was just like automatic drawing – it created art by chance. The marks were made subconsciously, with little control over the outcome.

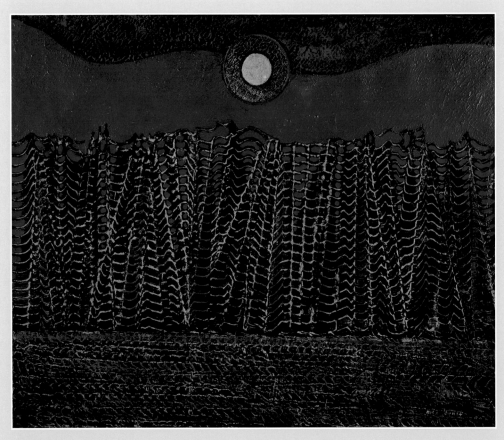

Fishbone Forest, Max Ernst, 1926

Look closer

Can you see how Ernst built up this textured forest by scraping off paint over the backbone of a fish?

Sand fish

André Masson experimented in his own way, by freely pouring streams of gesso (thin white paint) onto his canvas, then covering it with sand. He shook off the excess, then quickly drew around the shapes and added coloured paint straight from the tube. The sand picture below became a vicious fight between several razor-toothed fish. Masson often painted violent images, probably influenced by his experience of war.

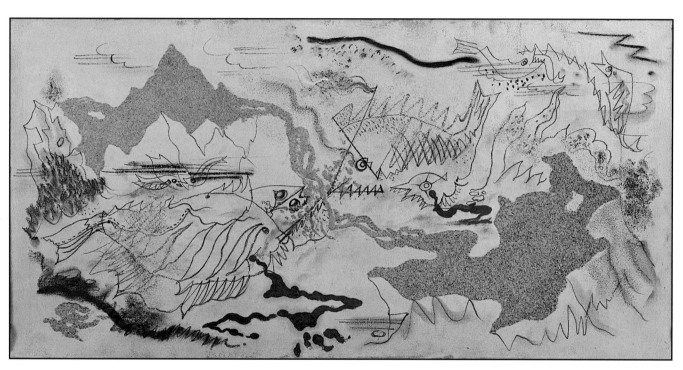

Battle of Fishes, André Masson, 1926

Smoke and scales

Later on, in the 1930s, two more artists developed 'accidental' techniques. Decalcomania, the brainchild of Oscar Domínguez, involved covering paper or glass with paint, pressing it onto canvas, then peeling it off again to reveal a bubbly or scaly texture. Wolfgang Paalen meanwhile invented fumage – making impressions with candle smoke on a canvas of wet paint.

Hyper-real dreams

At the opposite end of the scale to automatic painting, some Surrealists pictured their dreams, fears and hallucinations in a hyper-real style. They were still using the subconscious for inspiration, but painting it much more consciously!

Free world
The Surrealists believed that the subconscious mind provided a 'superior reality'. They saw it as its own free world, untouched by the rules of modern society. In a way it couldn't be 'brainwashed' by anyone's ideas or opinions. It existed independently, ticking away creatively behind the scenes.

Alien mindscapes
Yves Tanguy painted the subconscious as a very particular type of place. His haunting scenes look like alien planets or moonscapes, scattered with unidentifiable forms. Tanguy was an off-beat character who enjoyed being a Surrealist in all aspects of his life. At parties he would chew on socks or eat live spiders to shock people!

Look closer
This perplexing picture is made no clearer by its title, which Tanguy took from a psychiatric case file. What are your first impressions when you look at the painting?

Mama, Papa is Wounded!, Yves Tanguy, 1927

Danger on the Stairs, Pierre Roy, 1927-8

Dangerous dream

Combining the everyday with the unexpected was a favourite trick of Pierre Roy. Here he shows a familiar picture of a staircase, but all the comforts of home are riddled with danger. The snake turns the image into a nightmare, summoned by the subconscious. This deadly creature is slithering towards us ... will we wake up in time?

Hand-painted photographs

By 1929, dream paintings like these were becoming more common than automatic art. That year, a new and soon-to-be-famous artist – Salvador Dalí (see p.20) – arrived in Paris. Dalí described his pictures as 'hand-painted dream photographs'. He painted them as precisely as possible, to make his subconscious 'irrationality' look real.

A man with a moustache

Salvador Dalí was an outrageous showman who said his long, curled moustache was his 'antenna' to contact the universe! When he moved to Paris from Spain in 1929, his reputation came before him.

Frights on film

Paris already knew about Dalí thanks to his fellow Spaniards, Joan Miró and Luis Buñuel. Dalí came to Paris to help Buñuel make a film called *Un Chien Andalou (An Andalusian Dog)*. This turned out to be intensely surreal, with scenes including ants eating a hand and an armpit becoming a sea urchin! Dalí and Buñuel did their best to shock people – and they did, to the film's great success.

Daydreaming Dalí

Dalí's talent for art had started early – as a young boy in Spain. He was much more interested in painting than memorising things at school, and spent a lot of time daydreaming and imagining. At first Dalí admired traditional painting by old masters such as Diego Velázquez (1599-1660). Then the work of de Chirico (see p.9) caught his eye, and he entered the world of the improbable.

Salvador Dalí

Fears and fantasies

When Dalí moved to Paris, he soon became an active member of the Surrealist group. He was fascinated by Freud (see p.8) and allegedly ate lots of cheese before going to bed to give himself vivid dreams! Dalí painted certain things very often, including swarming ants, crutches, elephants and eggs. They all became symbols of his own fears and fantasies, dredged from his unconscious mind.

Melting time

The melting clocks in *The Persistence of Memory* (below) were another favourite symbol of Dalí's. He said they were inspired by a particularly ripe Camembert cheese! They flop and ooze in a beach-like setting, wilting in the heat of the sun. Nearby a pocket-watch is crawling with ants – Dalí seems to be confronting the way we are ruled by time. Here in this eerie memory or dreamscape, time doesn't matter and recording it is useless.

The Persistence of Memory, Salvador Dalí, 1931

Look closer

Dalí's realistic style tricks us into relating this to the world we know. What other things here look ordinary but strange at the same time?

"At the age of six I wanted to be a cook. At seven I wanted to be Napoleon. And my ambition has been growing steadily ever since."

Salvador Dalí

The picture trickster

In traditional painting, when you look at an image, you can usually understand it straight away. When you look at a picture by René Magritte, it seems straightforward – but you need to look twice!

Belgian background

Magritte was a Belgian who lived in Paris for a few years until 1930. At that point he had an argument with André Breton and moved back home to Brussels. He had worked there as a poster and wallpaper designer, which contributed to his neat, graphic style. But Magritte was a Surrealist at heart, and a master of making things we recognise look nonsensical.

Picture paradox

A Magritte painting is a bit like a brainteaser, full of visual tricks and paradox. Paradox is something that contradicts itself – for example, a hot ice cube. Magritte loved putting together objects and figures that had no relationship to each other. He would also disrupt the scale of things or set them in unexpected places.

The Human Condition, René Magritte, 1933

A picture or a tree?

The Human Condition is a painting within a painting, though that's not immediately obvious! We're looking at a scene through a window that's partly hidden by the same scene on an artist's canvas. Magritte liked the idea that the tree is both inside the room and outside. He compared it to the way we see things – for example, we have a picture in our head that looks like a tree but isn't the tree itself.

········▶ ## *Look closer*

The writing on this painting means 'This is not a pipe'. Can you see what Magritte was doing here?

The Treachery of Images, René Magritte, 1929

Clairvoyance, René Magritte, 1936

Seeing the future

This is a painting of Magritte himself painting – but it is more than just a self-portrait. He is painting an egg, laid on a table, while on his canvas there's a bird. The title of this picture is *Clairvoyance*, which means 'looking into the future'. The artist knows subconsciously that an egg hatches into a bird, so he is one step ahead of what his eyes see!

Photo play

A photograph captures an image of the real world – so how can it be surreal? This was a problem that many photographers solved, using imaginative techniques and effects.

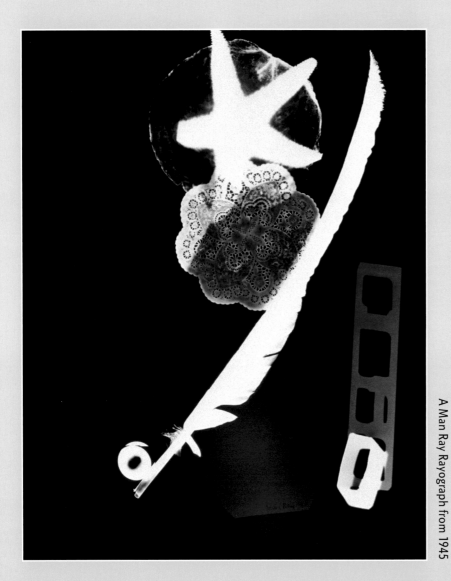

A Man Ray Rayograph from 1945

Picture tricks

Photography was already nearly a hundred years old when the Surrealists were working. Scientists were learning about colour processing, though most photos were still black and white. There was no such thing as a digital camera or image-editing software. But the Surrealists experimented with other methods to make their pictures look otherworldly or mysterious.

Man Rayographs

When is a photograph not a photograph? When it's a Rayograph! Man Ray was one of the leading Surrealist photographers, and he invented this way of making photos without a camera. He would lay random objects, like this feather, doily and starfish, on photographic paper, expose the paper to light and develop it. The result made real things look abstract and confusing, just as the Surrealists liked them.

Eerie accident

One day Man Ray was working in his dark room with fellow photographer Lee Miller (see p.32). One of them accidentally turned on a light – something you shouldn't do when a photo is developing. Photographers had made this mistake before, but for the Surrealists it was exciting! It solarised the image, so that light areas appeared dark and dark areas light. You can see an example of this in Hans Bellmer's doll photo (right).

(see p.32)

Look closer

Can you see how the shadows are light, and vice versa? What effect does this have? Why do you think the Surrealists liked it?

The Doll, Hans Bellmer, 1934-35

The Simulator, Dora Maar, 1936

Twisted images

Montage (like collage) was another technique that helped photographers turn reality into dream-like visions. For the image on the left, Dora Maar photographed a vaulted ceiling, painted out the windows and turned the print upside down. Then she glued on a cut-out picture of a boy and photographed the whole thing together. The result is dizzying and baffling, because it looks like a single photo!

Unordinary objects

'As beautiful as the chance encounter of a sewing machine and an umbrella on an operating table.' This line was published in 1869, by the poet Comte de Lautréamont – but it perfectly anticipated the idea of Surrealist objects.

Disclocated things

The Surrealists called Lautréamont their prophet because he seemed to foresee their ideas. Man Ray even made an object in his honour, showing exactly what is described in the quote above. The term 'object' means just that – a thing, turned into art. The Surrealists took objects from their usual settings and linked them to things that they had no connection to.

A photo of Meret Oppenheim's *Breakfast in Fur*, 1936

Fur in a teacup

Flea markets were the ideal places to pick up material for Surrealist objects. The artists went shopping, buying cheap, usually mass-produced items. Then they destroyed the objects' normal use, as you can see in the images on this page. Lining a teacup with furry material made it very unappealing to drink out of!

Lobster talk

In many ways, Surrealist objects were similar to Dada readymades (see p.7). But Breton believed that only the subconscious could dream up such bewildering things. How would it feel to pick up a lobster telephone and hold it to your ear? Would you even dare to? Something like this is so unlikely that it's both funny and menacing at the same time.

"I do not understand why, when I ask for a grilled lobster in a restaurant, I am never served a cooked telephone."

Salvador Dalí

Lobster Telephone, Salvador Dalí, 1936

This is cheese

In 1936, Breton and friends held an Exhibition of Surrealist Objects in Paris. It included Magritte's *This is a Piece of Cheese* – a small painting of a slice of cheese, placed under the glass lid of a real cheese tray. It was the puzzling opposite of *The Treachery of Images* (*This is not a Pipe*; see p.23), because this time the picture declared it *was* cheese! At the end of the exhibition, the cheese tray was returned to its everyday use.

Furniture face

A beautiful lady with big red lips, long eyelashes and wavy blonde hair – this was Mae West, a famous American film actress, but Dalí pictured her face as a room!

Face of Mae West Which May be Used as a Surrealist Apartment, Salvador Dalí, 1934–5

From woman to wall

West was a superstar in the 1930s, and Dalí found her captivating. He decided to celebrate her beauty with a surreal collage. He cut up a magazine photo of the actress, then added paint and other details to transform her face into a fancy apartment. She has curtain hair, picture eyes, a fireplace nose and a sofa for lips!

In 1974, an architect helped to translate Dalí's collage into an actual room. Visitors can still see it at the Dalí Theatre-Museum in Figueres, Spain.

Double images

In the early 1930s, Dalí developed what he called his paranoiac-critical method. He would force himself into a paranoid state, where he felt irrationally distrustful of the world around him. This, he said, helped him to see links between things that aren't logically connected. It led him to create double images, where objects can be interpreted in different ways – for example, a sofa or lips in this picture.

"I am the first to be surprised and often terrified by the images I see appear upon my canvas."
Salvador Dalí

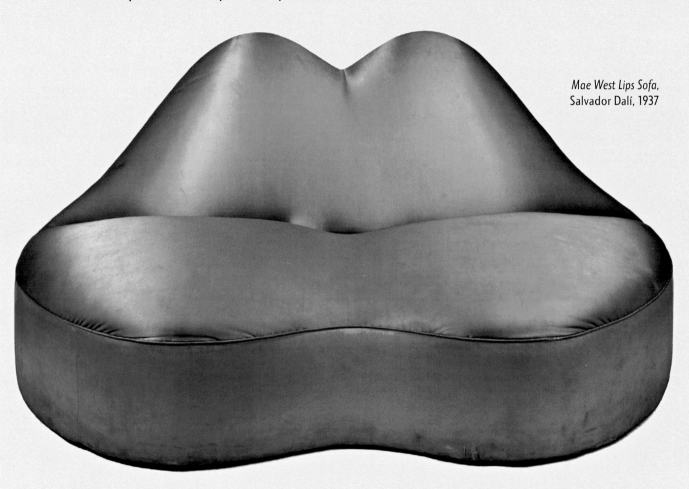

Mae West Lips Sofa,
Salvador Dalí, 1937

Lips to sit on

Dalí went further with those sofa lips – he replicated them as real sofas! The idea actually came from an eccentric Englishman called Edward James, who was a great patron to the Surrealists. He had a huge collection of their work and helped to design the sofas for his own Surrealist home, Monkton House in Sussex. It was full of bizarre designs and deliberately shocking Surrealist objects.

Wacky designs

Dalí soon got a taste for designing furniture, interiors and even clothes. Sometimes he collaborated with other designers, including the fashion icon Elsa Schiaparelli. He created a dress with drawers, a shoe hat, a chair with hands and some wacky shop window displays. Another design was for a hotel nightclub in the shape of a sea urchin – but it never went ahead!

Surrealist showtime

Pictures on a gallery wall were one thing – but Surrealist exhibitions tended to be off the wall too. The Surrealists loved putting on a show that would throw their visitors into startling situations and make as many headlines as possible.

A report showing the opening event of the First International Surrealist Exhibition

Harbour and Room, Paul Nash, 1932-6

London 1936
The first International Surrealist Exhibition took place in London in 1936. It was organised by a collection of English artists, along with the Paris group. On opening day, crowds gathered in Trafalgar Square to find a lady performing in a wedding dress with her head hidden inside a flower arrangement (above)! Later Dalí gave a lecture wearing a diving suit, but minutes into it he started to suffocate and had to be prised out.

English eccentrics
The poster for the London exhibition declared, 'Surrealism Has Arrived'. The show helped to publicise many English Surrealists, including Paul Nash (left), Eileen Agar (see p.33) and Roland Penrose (p.43). British writers also featured, such as the Welsh poet Dylan Thomas who greeted visitors with a teacup of boiled string, asking if they'd like it weak or strong!

⟶ *Look closer*
Paul Nash painted a room blending into a harbour. Which parts of the scene make sense, and which make it surreal? Look at the scale of things as well as the positioning of the water.

Paris 1938

Two years later, the Surrealists chose Paris for their next international exhibition. This time, Dalí's *Rainy Taxi* was parked in the forecourt. It had a doll driver whose head was trapped in a shark's mouth, and a shop mannequin passenger wearing an evening dress and snails. After passing this exhibit, visitors walked through a corridor lined with more mannequins, each one 'dressed' surreally by a different artist.

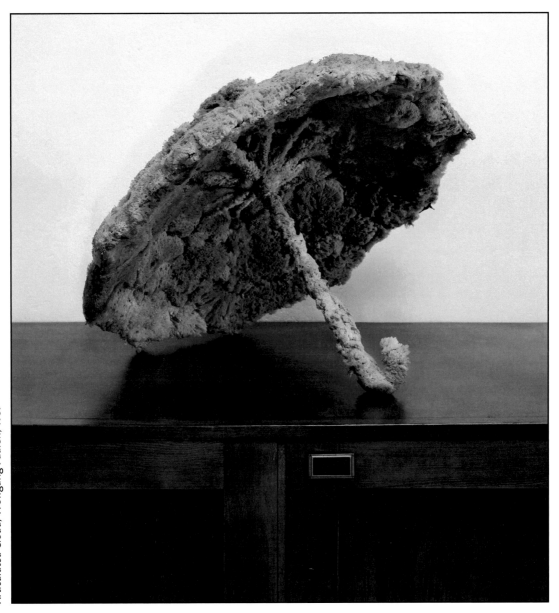

Articulated Cloud, Wolfgang Paalen, 1937

Silly success

The main room of the 1938 exhibition was dimly lit, so people were handed torches to help them see. There were leaves and mud all over the floor, a pond, four beds, 1,200 coal sacks hanging from the ceiling, and endless other artworks including Wolfgang Paalen's *Articulated Cloud* – an umbrella covered with sponges. The press found the whole show ridiculous and slated it, but the Surrealists saw this as a sign of success!

Woman and women

Breton described the idea of 'woman' as 'the most marvellous and disturbing problem in the world'. Surrealism celebrated everything about the female, though female artists in the movement still took second place to their male peers.

Female sleepers

Art in those days was a man's world, as it had been for centuries. But opportunities for women to study and make art did improve in the first decades of the 20th century. Many female artists became involved with the Surrealists, creatively, romantically and as muses. You can see four of them fast asleep in this photo by Roland Penrose!

Four Women Asleep, Lee Miller, Leonora Carrington, Ady Fidelin and Nusch Eluard, Lambe Creek, Cornwall, England, by Roland Penrose, 1937

Miller and Oppenheim

The photographer Lee Miller (see p.25) and artist Meret Oppenheim (p.26) were two famous female members of the group. Miller, an American, modelled for Man Ray in Paris and soon started producing her own Surrealist work. Oppenheim also modelled for Ray and went on to create object art. She loved manipulating household items, including a pair of boots joined at the toe and fur gloves with painted wooden fingers peeping out!

Carrington

Leonora Carrington met Max Ernst in London and moved back to Paris with him. (Later Ernst married another great female Surrealist, Dorothea Tanning). Carrington painted this self-portrait aged just 20, perched stiffly on a chair in a dreamlike setting. There's a hyena beside her and a rocking horse floating behind. Is the white horse outside the window the same creature, come to life?

Self Portrait, Leonora Carrington, 1937–8

Angel of Anarchy, Eileen Agar, 1936–40

Agar's Angel

This fabric-wrapped head, both pretty and sinister, was created by the British artist Eileen Agar. She used the Surrealist trick of double meaning – for example, are these feathers on a headdress or do they represent hair? Agar also made hats for Surrealist occasions – she loved the playful side of the style, and the fact that the women looked elegant even when they were being rebellious!

My **twin** self

A woman sits next to herself on a bench, in front of a dark, stormy sky. Each version of her has half a heart, linked to its other half by a long blood vessel. This strange twin person is Frida Kahlo, a Mexican artist famous for her self-portraits.

Frida Kahlo and her husband Diego Rivera

Inside out

Kahlo said she never knew she was a Surrealist, 'until André Breton came to Mexico and told me I was one.' What she did know was that she painted her own states of mind, her emotions and her inner reality. Breton deeply admired this inside-outness and called her work 'a ribbon around a bomb.' Underneath the surface, there was a lot going on!

"I paint my own reality. The only thing I know is that I paint because I need to, and I paint whatever passes through my head without any other consideration."

Frida Kahlo

Emotional anguish

What do you see when you look at the painting *The Two Fridas* (right)? The Frida on the left is trying to clamp the artery, but the blood keeps dripping down on her white dress. The other Frida is holding a tiny picture – of her former husband, the artist Diego Rivera. Kahlo painted this after they divorced, putting all the pain she was feeling down on canvas.

Imaginary friend

In her diary, Kahlo said this double image stemmed from a childhood memory of an imaginary friend. It was as if a conscious part of her had found an unconscious part to talk to – a surreal idea in itself. The painting is also full of contradictions, between the upright 'rational' Frida doing her best to stop the bleeding, and the emotional Frida driven by her subconscious, clinging on to what she has lost.

Damaged life

Kahlo painted the broken heart very realistically. She was all too familiar with the human body, having spent a lot of time in hospital. As a child she had polio, which deformed her right leg, then aged 18 she suffered a near-fatal bus accident that affected her for the rest of her life. It was while she was recovering from one of many operations that Kahlo took up painting.

The Two Fridas, Frida Kahlo, 1939

35

Anguish and exile

Horrific times began to unfold in Europe in the 1930s. First came the Spanish Civil War (1936–39) and then the outbreak of the Second World War (1939–45). Artists soon fled to safer places, and New York took over from Paris as the global capital of art.

Degenerate art

Most of the Surrealists were socialists, strongly opposed to undemocratic powers like Hitler's Nazi Party in Germany and Franco's Nationalists in Spain. Hitler wanted control over all aspects of life and punished modern artists, calling them 'degenerate'. Many works of art were confiscated or destroyed, including ones by Dalí, Miró and Ernst.

Refuge in America

When Nazi troops began to occupy France, life in Paris changed. Many artists, facing hostility, returned to their native countries or fled to the USA or Mexico. As a German, Ernst was arrested by the French and held in prison camps with other 'enemy' artists. Later he escaped and took refuge in the USA, with the help of American gallery owner Peggy Guggenheim.

The First Papers of Surrealism exhibition in New York, 1942, featuring *16 Miles of String* by Marcel Duchamp

A new HQ

New York soon became the Surrealists' new HQ, with Guggenheim playing an important part in promoting them. They held exhibitions, including First Papers of Surrealism in 1942 (left). At the opening, children were asked to run round playing catch and hopscotch while Marcel Duchamp's *16 Miles of String* (left) festooned the whole gallery space. As usual, it brought the Surrealists attention.

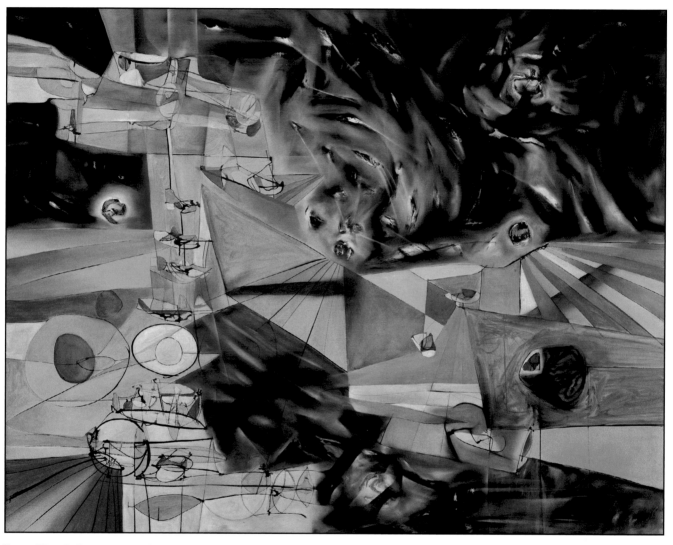

Years of Fear, Roberto Matta, 1941

Painted horrors

Many Surrealists made work in response to the terror and devastation of war. One was Roberto Matta, a Chilean artist who had lived in Paris and then became part of the New York group. He called his paintings 'inscapes', or maps of the unknowing mind. This one, with all its dark explosions, has a feeling of the end of the world.

Look closer

Why do you think Matta described his images as 'inscapes'?
What sort of place does this painting remind you of, and why?

Wonders after **war**

Surrealism managed to survive the Second World War, though the group as a whole was damaged. Some artists were expelled or detached themselves, while others carried on developing their own styles.

The Surrealist, Victor Brauner, 1947

Paris 1947

Breton and others returned to Paris and continued to drive the movement there. To mark their comeback, they staged an international exhibition, 'Surrealism in 1947'. This time the focus was on magic and the supernatural, freeing the mind from earthly reality. The show featured a Hall of Superstitions, a series of altars dedicated to mythical beings and a mass of other mysterious works by Surrealists old and new.

Tables and tarot

Victor Brauner was one artist who showed his work at the 1947 exhibition. It included a statue with one head and three bodies, a 'Wolftable' with the stuffed head and tail of a fox, and the images such as the above, based on a tarot card. The idea of cards giving people psychic powers intrigued the Surrealists – Brauner and others had already designed a full deck of tarot-inspired cards several years before.

Avida Dollars

Many Surrealist masters went their own way after the war. Dalí stayed in the USA until 1948. He had made a lot of money there – Breton accused him of being greedy and called him Avida Dollars ('mad about dollars'), an anagram of his real name! Dalí loved being a celebrity and even worked in Hollywood, designing dream-scene sets for Alfred Hitchcock's 1945 film *Spellbound*, as well as a storyboard for Walt Disney.

The Ugly Duckling, Salvador Dalí, 1966

Miró's public art

Joan Miró travelled to the USA for the first time in 1947. There he created an enormous mural for a hotel in Cincinnati, described by a critic as 'spontaneous and exuberant … like music heard through a summer window'. Later, Miró also experimented with ceramics and sculpture in his colourful, childlike style. You can see examples of his work in many public places in Paris, Spain and the USA.

Miró's *Woman and Bird* statue in Barcelona

Look closer

Dalí went on to illustrate several books, including *Alice's Adventures in Wonderland* and Hans Christian Andersen's fairy tales. This illustration shows a scene from *The Ugly Duckling*. What is Surreal about it? Compare it to Dalí's painting on p.5.

A bowler hat and apples

A man stands stiffly in a bowler hat, with a calm sea stretching out behind him. We can't see his face because an apple is hiding it! Apples and bowler hats were the things that Magritte (see p.22) became most famous for.

Son of Man, René Magritte, 1964

Somebody or nobody

Magritte was not a showman like Dalí. He wore sensible clothes – an overcoat and bowler hat – and lived an orderly life, preferring to be anonymous. This is probably a self-portrait, but the man's face won't give it away. Magritte's bowler-hatted figures are always impersonal, as if the person is an object. They represent a conventional, middle-class 'somebody' whom we never get to know.

René Magritte

Seen but hidden

Magritte loved the idea that we can't see what we know is there. The bright green apple becomes like a mask, with only the hint of an eye visible behind it. Magritte painted other figures with a bird, pipe or flowers concealing their features too. Sometimes the bowler-hatted man was just an open shape, like a stencil, with a sky or other scenery painted inside it.

Fruitful fruit

As for apples, Magritte painted them repeatedly – wearing carnival masks, hovering over landscapes, declaring they are not apples, and so on. One day he gave an apple picture to Paul McCartney of the Beatles, with 'Au Revoir' (Goodbye) written across it. The band used a similar apple as the logo for their famous record label, which may have inspired Steve Jobs and his Apple Computers!

Shrinking potion

In the painting below, a giant apple fills up a room wall to wall. Imagine taking a bite – where would your tooth marks be? Like other Surrealists, Magritte was fascinated by the book *Alice's Adventures in Wonderland*, written by Lewis Carroll in 1865. This mighty fruit makes us feel as if we've taken a shrinking potion, straight from this popular story.

The Listening Room, René Magritte, 1952

𝓛ook closer

Magritte liked to make conundrums with the titles of his paintings, as well as the pictures themselves. Why do you think this is called *The Listening Room*? Who is doing the listening? What is there to be heard?

Globally surreal

From the beginning, André Breton campaigned to make Surrealism a global movement – and he succeeded! It wasn't long before the 'revolution of the mind' had spread around Europe and reached Japan, Mexico, Egypt, Australia and beyond.

Conquering the world

Breton published international magazines and bulletins and held lectures and exhibitions abroad. Surrealist artists also travelled, and outsiders came to Paris and took ideas back home. By the mid-1930s, the unconscious was being unravelled by excited writers and artists around the world.

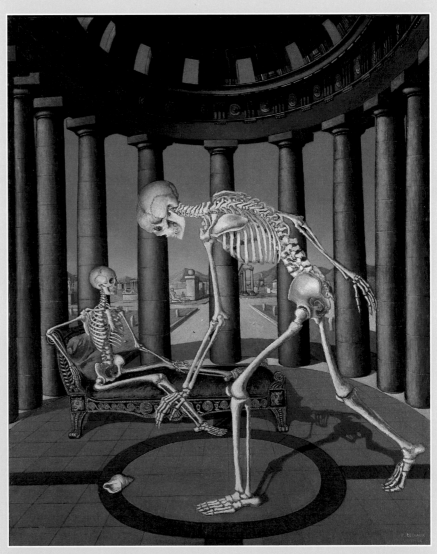

The Skeleton Has the Shell, Paul Delvaux, 1944

Belgian skeletons

Paul Delvaux was a Belgian painter with a Magritte-like illustrative style. He liked to show surprising encounters and people in unexpected places. Not many things are more unlikely than living skeletons, picking up seashells in an ancient town! This painting has the unsettling feeling of a dream, where things from different times and places come together.

Gorky in New York

The American-Armenian Arshile Gorky discovered Surrealism in New York. Breton claimed Gorky's *The Liver is the Cock's Comb* was 'one of the most important paintings made in America.' It is an imaginary world with loose links to reality, showing the influence of Miró in its colourful, ambiguous forms. Gorky's work in turn had a key impact on the development of Abstract Expressionism (see p.44).

The Liver is the Cock's Comb, Arshile Gorky, 1944

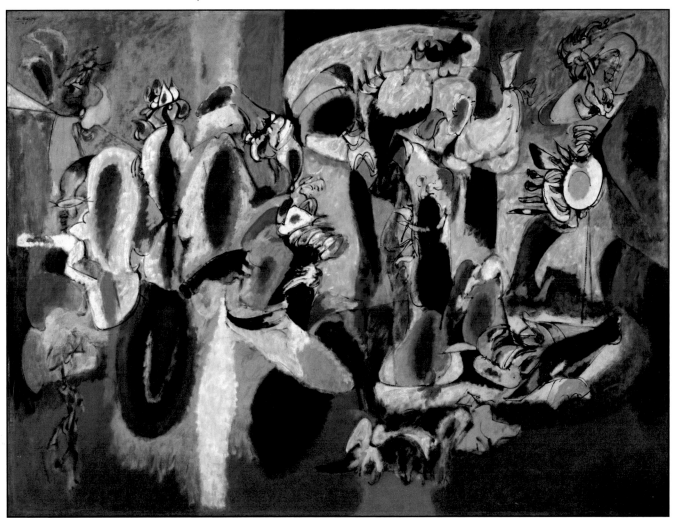

From England to Egpyt

In England, Roland Penrose opened a gallery to promote the Surrealists. He was a leading artist himself, and married Lee Miller (see p.32) who had previously lived in Cairo. This opened links between the English Surrealists and Egypt, where an Art and Liberty group formed in 1938, in opposition to Hitler's attack on modern art (see p.36). Egyptian artists developed their own versions of Surrealism, helped by Miller who introduced them to games and ideas for tapping into the subconscious.

Legacy of the unexpected

Once the Surrealists had unlocked the unconscious, it would never be locked up again! The movement lost its driving force when Breton died in 1966, but it stayed alive in the minds of generations to come.

Abstract accidents

Art changed steadily during the Second World War, when the creative capital shifted from Paris to New York (see p.36). Painters there took the Surrealists' ideas on board but steered them towards a new style called Abstract Expressionism. Jackson Pollock was particularly interested in painting 'automatically' or 'accidentally'. He developed a method known as 'action painting', where he threw, dripped and drizzled paint onto his canvas.

Jackson Pollock 'action painting' in 1960

Uncanny Pop

In the 1960s, Pop artists such as Andy Warhol and Claes Oldenburg rebelled against the seriousness of Abstract Expressionism. Like many Surrealists, they began taking ordinary objects and giving them a new context or impact. The idea of a giant ice cream melting on the roof of a building (top right) is as uncanny and unlikely as a bright green apple filling a room! Oldenburg magnified everyday things to confront our way of seeing art.

Dropped Cone, Claes Oldenburg and Coosje van Bruggen, 2001

Film and fantasy

Surrealism gave new importance to fantasy and the imagination, a world where common sense has little meaning. Filmmakers from Hitchcock (see p.39) to Tim Burton (see below) have used this to their advantage. Modern-day advertising is also full of surreal images, because they make us look twice and remember them! These days it is easy to manipulate an image digitally and make it look impossible or dreamlike.

Concepts for the future

Like many art movements of the 20th century, Surrealism challenged the idea of 'high art'. It helped to pave the way for something more conceptual – making the idea behind an artwork more important than the way it looks or how it is made. Surrealism was also often humorous, thought-provoking, mysterious or just fun! All this made it accessible to ordinary people – and unforgettable, too.

Tim Burton's film *Edward Scissorhands* (1990) is a surreal cross between a dream and a nightmare.

Glossary

abstract – not representing an actual object, place or living thing

Abstract Expressionism – an art movement in the USA (1940s–50s), based on creating art for emotional effect

ambiguous – unclear

automatic drawing – letting the hand draw spontaneously

automatism – doing things without conscious thought

canvas – a strong type of fabric that many artists use to paint on

collaborate – work together

collage – an artwork made by sticking bits of paper, fabric or other materials onto a surface

conceptual – based on ideas, or concepts

conscious – aware; knowing what is happening

contradictions – things that are opposite to one another

conundrum – a riddle or puzzle

Cubists – artists such as Pablo Picasso who made images using geometric shapes and multiple viewpoints (1907–1920s)

Dada – a movement (1916–24) that aimed to destroy traditions in art, with often nonsensical work

degenerate – immoral

eccentric – unconventional

elitist – seemingly superior to others

flea market – a street market selling second-hand items

hallucination – the experience of seeing or sensing something that doesn't exist in reality

hypnosis – a sleep-like state

manipulate – control or influence something

mural – a painting made directly onto a wall

muse – a person who inspires an artist

neurological – to do with the nerves and the brain

paranoid – intensely suspicious or anxious about being harmed

patron – a person who supports someone else financially

photomontage – a collage made from photographs

polio – a disease that can paralyse or deform parts of the body

Pop artists – a group of artists in the UK and USA (1950s–70s) who drew inspiration from popular culture and commercial imagery

provocative – deliberately causing a reaction such as shock or anger

psychiatrist – a doctor specialising in mental health

rational – based on reason or logic

replicate – to copy something

scale – the size of things in relation to one another

socialist – believing in a social system whereby a country's goods and services are owned and shared by the public

solarise – reverse light and dark parts of a photograph

storyboard – a series of drawings representing the shots planned for a film or TV production

subconscious – the part of our brain that is responsible for feelings and things we do automatically or without knowing it

supernatural – things that are thought to exist beyond the visible universe, such as spirits or ghosts

superstition – belief in something that is considered irrational, such as magic or the supernatural

symbol – a thing that represents, or stands for, something else

texture – the feel of a surface, such as rough brick or smooth glass

trance – a semi-conscious state

traumatised – emotionally wounded or distressed

Find out more

Books
Imagine That!: Activities and Adventures in Surrealism (Art Explorers) by Joyce Raimondo (Watson-Guptill, 2004)

Getting to Know the World's Greatest Artists: Dalí by Mike Venezia (Scholastic, 2015)

Websites
www.moma.org/learn/moma_learning/themes/surrealism

Information and activities from the New York Museum of Modern Art (MoMA), including 'write your own manifesto'

www.tate.org.uk/art/art-terms/s/surrealism

An overview of Surrealism by the Tate Modern gallery in London.

They also have a kids' page
http://www.tate.org.uk/kids/explore/who-is/who-salvador-dali

The Tate Kids' page on Salvador Dalí

www.renemagritte.org

Biography, quotes and masterpieces of René Magritte

Timeline

1865 Lewis Carroll writes *Alice's Adventures in Wonderland* (see p.39), which later inspires many Surrealists.

1900 Sigmund Freud publishes *The Interpretation of Dreams*, a book about the subconscious.

1912 The Cubists Pablo Picasso and Georges Braque invent collage.

1914 The First World War begins. Max Ernst, André Masson and others are drafted to fight. André Breton works on a psychiatric ward in France, treating victims of shell-shock.

1916 The Dada movement is founded.

1918 The First World War ends.

1919 Breton experiments with automatic writing. He publishes the surrealist magazine, *Littérature*.

1920 The last major Dada exhibition takes place in Cologne, Germany.

1921 Breton visits Freud in Austria.

1924 Breton publishes his first *Surrealist Manifesto* and launches the Surrealist magazine *La Révolution Surréaliste*.

1925 The first Surrealist exhibition takes place in Paris. Joan Miró has a solo exhibition. Ernst discovers frottage (rubbing; see p.16).

1926 Man Ray makes a Surrealist film, *Emak Bakia (Leave Me Alone)*. The Belgian Surrealist group is formed.

1927 René Magritte moves to Paris from Belgium.

1928 Breton publishes his book *Surrealism and Painting*.

1929 Salvador Dalí moves to Paris. He and Luis Buñuel release the film *Un Chien Andalou*.

1930 Breton publishes his second *Surrealist Manifesto*. The magazine *Surrealism in the Service of the Revolution* is founded. Magritte returns to live in Belgium.

1933 The Surrealist magazine *Minotaure* is first issued. Adolf Hitler and his Nazi Party in Germany start to demolish collections of modern or 'degenerate' art.

1935 The first *International Bulletin of Surrealism* is published in Prague, Czechoslovakia (now the Czech Republic).

1936 The first exhibition of Surrealist objects takes place in Paris. An International Surrealist exhibition is shown in London.

1937 The Nazi Party organises a scathing Degenerate Art exhibition in Munich, Germany.

1938 International Surrealist exhibitions happen in Paris and Amsterdam. Breton travels to Mexico, which he describes as 'the most Surrealist country in the world'. He arranges a solo exhibition for Frida Kahlo in New York, USA. The Art and Liberty group forms in Cairo, Egypt.

1939 The Second World War begins. Many Surrealists move to New York.

1942 The First Papers of Surrealism exhibition takes place in New York. The Surrealist *VVV* and *DYN* magazines are launched.

1945 Dalí designs dream scenes for Alfred Hitchcock's film *Spellbound*.

1947 Breton and Marcel Duchamp organise an International Surrealist exhibition in Paris. Miró visits the USA.

1948 Dalí returns to Spain from the USA.

1954 Kahlo dies in Mexico.

1966 Breton dies in Paris.

1967 Magritte dies in Belgium.

1969 Dalí illustrates *Alice in Wonderland* (see p.39).

1974 The Dalí Theatre-Museum opens in Figueres, Spain (see p.28).

1976 Max Ernst dies in Paris.

1983 Miró dies in Majorca.

1989 Dalí dies in Spain.

Index

Impressionism

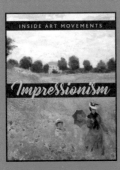

INSIDE ART MOVEMENTS

Impressionism

Renaissance

INSIDE ART MOVEMENTS

The Renaissance

Surrealism

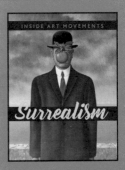

INSIDE ART MOVEMENTS

Surrealism

Cubism

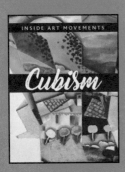

INSIDE ART MOVEMENTS

Cubism

Pop Art

INSIDE ART MOVEMENTS

Campbell's CONDENSED Pop Art TOMATO SOUP

Romanticism

INSIDE ART MOVEMENTS

Romanticism